I Am Me.
I Am One.

By Ablavi L. de Souza-Hughton

WTL INTERNATIONAL

I AM ME. I AM ONE.

Copyright © 2023 Ablavi de Souza-Hughton

Artwork by Cutie Fruity by WTL International

All rights reserved. No part of this publication may be reproduced in any form or by any electronic or mechanical means, including information storage and material systems, except in the case of brief quotations embodied in critical articles or reviews, without permission in writing from its publisher,
WTL International.

Published by
WTL International
930 North Park Drive
P.O.Box 33049
Brampton, Ontario
L6S 6A7 Canada
www.wtlipublishing.com

978-1-7386309-9-8

Printed in the U.S.A.

I am me. I am one.

In class at school, I have friends, but I miss my brother.
I wait for break time to go outside and play.
When we are together, he is silly.
He throws sticks into the air,
makes funny faces and sings very loud.

At break time, I see my brother.
My brother sees me.
We are two.

He runs around and makes a loud, buzzing sound.
He tells me he can now spell "buzzing bee."
B-u-z-z-i-n-g b-e-e

When school is over, my brother sees me again,
and we are happy.
We look for our sister.
She is walking under the big mango tree.
Her bag is open and flappy.

Our sister sees us. We are three.
We cheer her up because she is sad. Her arm hurts.

We see Mom, and Mom sees us. We are four.

We walk with Mom to the car, and we are glad.

We see Dad in the car, and Dad sees us. Now we are five.

We get home, and we are all together again. My family!

After a snack, we drove to town.
We dropped my sister off at our grandma's house.
My sister says goodbye to us. Now we are four.

Dad drives my brother to Boy Scouts.
My brother says goodbye to us. Now we are three.

Mom wants to stop and buy some fish from the fish market.
She says to Dad, "Pick me up on your way home."
I say bye to Mom. Now we are two.

Dad drops me off at my Adowa dance class.
Dad looks at me and says, "I will pick you up after work."

Now, I am me.
I am one, but I am not scared because in Adowa dance class,
I learn to be brave.
I learn to dance like one of the queen mothers of long ago.
I am me. I am one, and I am brave!

THE END

AUTHOR'S NOTE:

I AM ME. I AM ONE originated from a place of love and a longing for connection. The main character yearned to reunite with her biological family. Together with her siblings, they relied on each other, sharing whatever they each had to pull through the challenges of their parents' absence.
Endowed in traditional Kente cloth and beads, the protagonist gains strength and comfort from dancing Adowa, the traditional Akan dance from Ghana.

Kente cloth

Ghana flag

www.ingramcontent.com/pod-product-compliance
Lightning Source LLC
Chambersburg PA
CBHW061121170426
43209CB00013B/1631